By Joseph Brodsky

Nativity Poems

Translated by

MELISSA GREEN, SEAMUS HEANEY,

ANTHONY HECHT, GEORGE L. KLINE,

GLYN MAXWELL, PAUL MULDOON, ALAN MYERS,

DEREK WALCOTT, DANIEL WEISSBORT,

RICHARD WILBUR, AND THE AUTHOR

WITH PHOTOGRAPHS BY MIKHAIL LEMKHIN

Farrar, Straus and Giroux | NEW YORK

JOSEPH BRODSKY

Nativity Poems

FARRAR, STRAUS AND GIROUX
19 Union Square West, New York 10003

Distributed in Canada by Douglas & McIntyre Ltd.
Printed in the United States of America
Originally published, in slightly different form, in 1992 (revised 1996) by
Nezavisimaia Gazeta, Russia, as *Rozhdestvenskie stikhi*
Published in the United States by Farrar, Straus and Giroux
FIRST AMERICAN EDITION, 2001

Library of Congress Cataloging-in-Publication Data
Brodsky, Joseph, 1940–
  [Rozhdestvenskie stikhi. English & Russian]
  Nativity poems / Joseph Brodsky ; translated by Melissa Green . . .
[et al.].— Bilingual ed.
    p. cm.
  English and Russian.
  Also contains "A conversation with Joseph Brodsky" by Peter Vail.
  ISBN 0-374-21940-0 (hardcover : alk. paper)
  1. Brodsky, Joseph, 1940– —Translations into English. 2. Christmas—
Poetry. I. Vail', Petr, 1949– II. Green, Melissa. III. Brodsky, Joseph,
1940– . Rozhdestvo, tochka otscheta. English. IV. Title.

PG3479.4.R64 R6913 2001
891.71'44—dc21

                                            2001040435

Designed by Gretchen Achilles

Contents

Nativity Poems

РОЖДЕСТВЕНСКИЙ РОМАНС

ЕВГЕНИЮ РЕЙНУ, С ЛЮБОВЬЮ

Плывет в тоске необъяснимой
среди кирпичного надсада
ночной кораблик негасимый
из Александровского сада,
ночной фонарик нелюдимый,
на розу желтую похожий,
над головой своих любимых,
у ног прохожих.

Плывет в тоске необъяснимой
пчелиный хор сомнамбул, пьяниц.
В ночной столице фотоснимок
печально сделал иностранец,
и выезжает на Ордынку
такси с больными седоками,
и мертвецы стоят в обнимку
с особняками.

Плывет в тоске необъяснимой
певец печальный по столице,
стоит у лавки керосинной
печальный дворник круглолицый,
спешит по улице невзрачной
любовник старый и красивый.
Полночный поезд новобрачный
плывет в тоске необъяснимой.

CHRISTMAS BALLAD

FOR EVGENY REIN, WITH LOVE

There floats in an abiding gloom,
among immensities of brick,
a little boat of night: it seems
to sail through Alexander Park.
It's just a lonely streetlamp, though,
a yellow rose against the night,
for lovers strolling down below
    the busy street.

There floats in an abiding gloom
a drone of bees: men drunk, asleep.
In the dark capital a lone
tourist takes another snap.
Now out onto Ordynka turns
a taxicab, with sickly faces;
dead men lean into the arms
    of the low houses.

There floats in an abiding gloom
a poet in sorrow; over here
a round-faced man sells kerosene,
the sad custodian of his store.
Along a dull deserted street
an old Lothario hurries. Soon
the midnight-riding newlyweds
    sail through the gloom.

Плывет во мгле замоскворецкой
пловец в несчастие случайный,
блуждает выговор еврейский
на желтой лестнице печальной,
и от любви до невеселья
под Новый год, под воскресенье,
плывет красотка записная,
своей тоски не объясняя.

Плывет в глазах холодный вечер,
дрожат снежинки на вагоне,
морозный ветер, бледный ветер
обтянет красные ладони,
и льется мед огней вечерних
и пахнет сладкою халвою,
ночной пирог несет сочельник
над головою.

Твой Новый год по темно-синей
волне средь моря городского
плывет в тоске необъяснимой,
как будто жизнь начнется снова,
как будто будут свет и слава,
удачный день и вдоволь хлеба,
как будто жизнь качнется вправо,
качнувшись влево.

1962

There floats in outer Moscow one
who swims at random to his loss,
and Jewish accents wander down
a dismal yellow flight of stairs.
From love toward unhappiness,
to New Year's Eve, to Sunday, floats
a good-time girl: she can't express
  what's lost inside.

Cold evening floats within your eyes
and snow is fluttering on the panes
of carriages; the wind is ice
and pale, it seals your reddened palms.
Evening lights like honey seep;
the scent of halvah's everywhere,
as Christmas Eve lifts up its sweet-
  meats in the air.

Now drifting on a dark-blue wave
across the city's gloomy sea,
there floating by, your New Year's Eve—
as if life could restart, could be
a thing of light with each day lived
successfully, and food to eat,
—as if, life having rolled to left,
  it could roll right.

1962

TRANSLATED BY GLYN MAXWELL

1 ЯНВАРЯ 1965 ГОДА

Волхвы забудут адрес твой.
Не будет звезд над головой.
И только ветра сиплый вой
расслышишь ты, как встарь.
Ты сбросишь тень с усталых плеч,
задув свечу пред тем, как лечь,
поскольку больше дней, чем свеч,
сулит нам календарь.

Что это? Грусть? Возможно, грусть.
Напев, знакомый наизусть.
Он повторяется. И пусть.
Пусть повторится впредь.
Пусть он звучит и в смертный час,
как благодарность уст и глаз
тому, что заставляет нас
порою вдаль смотреть.

И молча глядя в потолок,
поскольку явно пуст чулок,
поймешь, что скупость—лишь залог
того, что слишком стар.
Что поздно верить чудесам.
И, взгляд подняв свой к небесам,
ты вдруг почувствуешь, что сам—
чистосердечный дар.

ЯНВАРЬ 1965

JANUARY 1, 1965

The kings will lose your old address.
No star will flare up to impress.
The ear may yield, under duress,
to blizzards' nagging roar.
The shadows falling off your back,
you'd snuff the candle, hit the sack,
for calendars more nights can pack
than there are candles for.

What is this? Sadness? Yes, perhaps.
A little tune that never stops.
One knows by heart its downs and ups.
May it be played on par
with things to come, with one's eclipse,
as gratefulness of eyes and lips
for what occasionally keeps
them trained on something far.

And staring up where no cloud drifts
because your sock's devoid of gifts
you'll understand this thrift: it fits
your age; it's not a slight.
It is too late for some breakthrough,
for miracles, for Santa's crew.
And suddenly you'll realize that you
yourself are a gift outright.

JANUARY 1965

TRANSLATED BY THE AUTHOR

РЕЧЬ О ПРОЛИТОМ МОЛОКЕ

I

1

Я пришел к Рождеству с пустым карманом.
Издатель тянет с моим романом.
Календарь Москвы заражен Кораном.
Не могу я встать и поехать в гости
ни к приятелю, у которого плачут детки,
ни в семейный дом, ни к знакомой девке.
Всюду необходимы деньги.
Я сижу на стуле, трясусь от злости.

2

Ах, проклятое ремесло поэта.
Телефон молчит, впереди диета.
Можно в месткоме занять, но это
—все равно, что занять у бабы.
Потерять независимость много хуже,
чем потерять невинность. Вчуже
полагаю, приятно мечтать о муже,
приятно произносить «пора бы».

SPEECH OVER SPILLED MILK

I

1

I arrive at Christmas without a kopeck.
The publisher's dragging on with my epic.
The Moscow calendar's going Islamic.
    I'm not going anywhere.
Not to the bawling kids of my buddy,
the family bosom, or a certain lady-
friend I know. They all cost money.
    I shake with ill will in my chair.

2

O, the damnable craft of the poet.
The phone doesn't ring, and the future? A diet.
I could scrounge at the union branch—you try it:
    may as well scrounge from the local girls.
Lost independence is worse by far
than lost innocence. To dream of a dear
hubby is awfully nice, I'm sure.
    How jolly, the jingle of wedding bells.

3

Зная мой статус, моя невеста
пятый год за меня ни с места;
и где она нынче, мне неизвестно:
правды сам черт из нее не выбьет.
Она говорит: «Не горюй напрасно.
Главное—чувства! Единогласно?»
И это с ее стороны прекрасно.
Но сама она, видимо, там, где выпьет.

4

Я вообще отношусь с недоверьем к ближним.
Оскорбляю кухню желудком лишним.
В довершенье всего досаждаю личным
взглядом на роль человека в жизни.
Они считают меня бандитом,
издеваются над моим аппетитом.
Я не пользуюсь у них кредитом.
«Наливайте ему пожиже!»

5

Я вижу в стекле себя холостого.
Я факта в толк не возьму простого,
как дожил до от Рождества Христова
Тысяча Девятьсот Шестьдесят Седьмого.
Двадцать шесть лет непрерывной тряски,
рытья по карманам, судейской таски,
ученья строить Закону глазки,
изображать немого.

3

Aware of my status, my fiancée
hasn't lifted a finger to marry me
these last five years. And where *is* she?

    The devil can't beat out that news.
She says, "Don't cry over nothing. What matters
are feelings. All in favor?" The vote is
carried. That's good of her. Clearly she favors

    finding a place she can score some booze.

4

In general I don't trust my fellows.
To the distaff side, my extra belly's
a burden. What I think man's role is

    never fails to piss them off.
They think of me as a kind of bandit,
mock my appetite, probably find it
funny. I certainly get no credit.

    "Pour him some of the watery stuff!"

5

I see my single self in a mirror.
I can make no sense of this simple data:
that I made it to Holy Christmas number

    nineteen hundred and sixty-seven.
Twenty-six years of continuous hassle,
digging in pockets, the blows of official
fists, performing the legal shuffle,

    flirting, faking I'm slow, unspeaking.

6

Жизнь вокруг идет как по маслу.
(Подразумеваю, конечно, массу.)
Маркс оправдывается. Но по Марксу
давно пора бы меня зарезать.
Я не знаю, в чью пользу сальдо.
Мое существование парадоксально.
Я делаю из эпохи сальто.
Извините меня за резвость!

7

То есть, все основания быть спокойным.
Никто уже не кричит «По коням!»
Дворяне выведены под корень.
Ни тебе Пугача, ни Стеньки.
Зимний взят, если верить байке.
Джугашвили хранится в консервной банке.
Молчит орудие на полубаке.
В голове моей—только деньги.

8

Деньги прячутся в сейфах, в банках,
в чулках, в полу, в потолочных балках,
в несгораемых кассах, в почтовых бланках.
Наводняют собой Природу!
Шумят пачки новеньких ассигнаций,
словно вершины берез, акаций.
Я весь во власти галлюцинаций.
Дайте мне кислороду!

6

Smoothly life slides by on its courses.
(Well, that's the case at least for the masses.)
Marx turns out to be right, but by Marx's
    lights mine should be out by now.
The balance is in who knows whose favor?
My living at all is a kind of dilemma.
I'm making a somersault out of my era.
    Pardon, please, this shiftless fellow.

7

It seems appropriate to stay calm.
Nobody's yelling at us: "*Aux armes!*"
The nobles have generally bought the farm.
    There's no Pugach or Stenka. "The Winter
Palace is ours!" So goes the plot.
Dzhugashvili's pickled for good in a pot.
The gun on the topgallant fo'c'sle's shot.
    I think, and only money enters.

8

Money hides in safes and strong rooms,
under the floor, in stockings, roof beams,
fireproof boxes, orders, tax forms,
    nature's gagging on all that green!
Freshly minted wads of cash are
rustling like the tops of acacias.
I'm foundering in hallucinations—
    somebody give me oxygen!

9

Ночь. Шуршание снегопада.
Мостовую тихо скребет лопата.
В окне напротив горит лампада.
Я торчу на стальной пружине.
Вижу только лампаду. Зато икону
я не вижу. Я подхожу к балкону.
Снег на крыши кладет попону,
и дома стоят, как чужие.

II

10

Равенство, брат, исключает братство.
В этом следует разобраться.
Рабство всегда порождает рабство.
Даже с помощью революций.
Капиталист развел коммунистов.
Коммунисты превратились в министров.
Последние плодят морфинистов.
Почитайте, что пишет Луций.

11

К нам не плывет золотая рыбка.
Маркс в производстве не вяжет лыка.
Труд не является товаром рынка.
Так говорить—оскорблять рабочих.
Труд—это цель бытия и форма.
Деньги—как бы его платформа.
Нечто помимо путей прокорма.
Размотаем клубочек.

9

Night. The rustle of falling snow.
The scratch of a spade on the stones below.
There's an icon lamp in an opposite window.

    Me, I'm wound on a spring of steel.
I can see the lamp, that's all. I can't actually
see the icon. Look from the balcony:
snow has saddled each roof with a canopy.

    Houses aren't themselves at all.

II

10

Equality, pal, throws brotherhood off.
Better make sense of that. A slave
breeds nothing but another slave,

    and no less after a revolution.
Capitalists breed communists,
who spawn in time careerists.
These finally hatch out *morphinists*.

    But all of this you find in Lucian.

11

The Goldfish swimming to and fro
will grant no wish. What did Marx know
about Production? Labor's no

    commodity. To say it is
insults the workers. It's the goal
and form of being. Money's, well,
its base. It's more than just a meal,

    but let's try making sense of this.

12

Вещи больше, чем их оценки.
Сейчас экономика просто в центре.
Объединяет нас вместо церкви,
объясняет наши поступки.
В общем, каждая единица
по своему существу—девица.
Она желает объединиться.
Брюки просятся к юбке.

13

Шарик обычно стремится в лузу.
(Я, вероятно, терзаю Музу.)
Не Конкуренции, но Союзу
принадлежит прекрасное завтра.
(Я отнюдь не стремлюсь в пророки.
Очень возможно, что эти строки
сократят ожиданья сроки:
«Год засчитывать за два».)

14

Пробил час и пора настала
для брачных уз Труда—Капитала.
Блеск презираемого металла
(дальше—изображенье в лицах)
приятней, чем пустота карманов,
проще, чем чехарда тиранов,
лучше цивилизации наркоманов,
общества, выросшего на шприцах.

12

Things are more than their worth in cash.
Economy's now on the topmost perch,
something to flock to other than church,
    explaining pretty much all we do.
Everyone, though, each separate person,
is really in essence a girl, a virgin
keen to unite—like your slacks imagine
    a skirt out there to go running to.

13

And a pool ball hopes to get to a pocket—
(I can hear my poor Muse wailing "Stop it!")
The bright tomorrow is not the Market.
    It's the one and only Union.
(Not that I'm trying to prophesy.
But these poor lines perhaps one day
will get the time reduced. Let's say,
    "Two years to be served as one.")

14

The time has come, the hour has chimed!
Let Work and Money be conjoined!
The muddy glint and gleam of coins,
    or later, faces worn by bills,
are preferable to empty pockets,
simpler than rotating despots,
smarter than a land of addicts
    raised on needles, schooled on pills.

15

Грех первородства—не суть сиротства.
Многим, бесспорно, любезней скотство.
Проще различье найти, чем сходство:
«У Труда с Капиталом контактов нету».
Тьфу-тьфу, мы выросли не в Исламе,
хватит трепаться о пополаме.
Есть влечение между полами.
Полюса создают планету.

16

Как холостяк я грущу о браке.
Не жду, разумеется, чуда в раке.
В семье есть ямы и буераки.
Но супруги—единственный тип владельцев
того, что они создают в усладе.
Им не требуется «не укради».
Иначе все пойдем Христа ради.
Поберегите своих младенцев!

17

Мне, как поэту, все это чуждо.
Больше: я знаю, что «коемуждо . . .».
Пишу и вздрагиваю: вот чушь-то,
неужто я против законной власти?
Время спасет, коль они неправы.
Мне хватает скандальной славы.
Но плохая политика портит нравы.
Это уж—по нашей части!

15

Original sin didn't orphan us.
Many prefer to be beasts. Likeness
is never as clear as difference. Thus:

    "Labor and Capital don't converge."
Touch wood, we're not Islamic yet.
Enough of things in separate beds.
The sexes seem inclined to wed.

    Two poles do tend to make an earth.

16

A single man, I long for the altar.
I don't expect a miracle up there.
Family life's no picnic, either.

    Mind, it's only man and wife
who get to own a thing through joy.
Thou Shalt Not Steal's unnecessary,
or we'd be beggars, by and by.

    Better keep your kiddies safe!

17

To me, a poet, it counts for nothing.
"To give to every man according . . ."
Writing this I jump: what roaring

    nonsense! Me? Against the powers?
Time preserve us if they're wrong.
I've infamy enough for one.
Bad politics makes morals turn.

    Now that's an old concern of ours.

18

Деньги похожи на добродетель.
Не падая сверху—Аллах свидетель—
деньги чаще летят на ветер
не хуже честного слова.
Ими не следует одолжаться.
С нами в гроб они не ложатся.
Им предписано умножаться,
словно в баснях Крылова.

19

Задние мысли сильней передних.
Любая душа переплюнет ледник.
Конечно, обществу проповедник
нужней, чем слесарь, науки.
Но, пока нигде не слыхать пророка,
предлагаю—дабы еще до срока
не угодить в объятья порока—
займите чем-нибудь руки.

20

Я не занят, в общем, чужим блаженством.
Это выглядит красивым жестом.
Я занят внутренним совершенством:
полночь—полбанки—лира.
Для меня деревья дороже леса.
У меня нет общего интереса.
Но скорость внутреннего прогресса
больше, чем скорость мира.

18

But Money's close to godliness.
It's not Heaven-sent—Allah attest—
and is just as keen to be gone with a gust
    of wind as, say, a promise is.
One shouldn't borrow the stuff, mind you.
It won't go where we're certain to.
And all it knows is two times two
    times two, as Krylov's fable says.

19

Thoughts held back hold more than those
one says aloud. Who can't outpace
a glacier? Times require of us
    no locksmith and no scientist
but a prophet! Since there isn't one
at home right now, to keep you from
the swift embrace of vice, a hands-on
    attitude's what I suggest.

20

I'm not concerned with others' bliss
in general—that's much too nice—
but to perfect the thing inside:
    midnight, drink, the lyre . . . What else?
The trees are dearer than the wood.
I share no interest with the crowd.
Inner progress has a speed
    much greater than the world itself.

21

Это—основа любой известной
изоляции. Дружба с бездной
представляет сугубо местный
интерес в наши дни. К тому же,
это свойство несовместимо
с братством, равенством и, вестимо,
благородством невозместимо,
недопустимо в муже.

22

Так, тоскуя о превосходстве,
как Топтыгин на воеводстве,
я пою вам о производстве.
Буде указанный выше способ
всеми правильно будет понят,
общество лучших сынов нагонит,
факел разума не уронит,
осчастливит любую особь.

23

Иначе—верх возьмут телепаты,
буддисты, спириты, препараты,
фрейдисты, неврологи, психопаты.
Кайф, состояние эйфории,
диктовать нам будет свои законы.
Наркоманы прицепят себе погоны.
Шприц повесят вместо иконы
Спасителя и Святой Марии.

21

All isolation stems from this.
Staying on terms with the abyss
is of strictly local interest
    these days. Such sensibilities
are out of tune with brotherhood,
equality, the common good;
gentility can't compensate;
    these are unmanly qualities.

22

Like Toptygin on his forest throne,
I yearn for the perfected thing.
I bash out my Production Song.
    For, should the means outlined herein
be fully grasped, society
will meet its brightest sons, bear high
the torch of reason. By and by
    it's happiness for everyone!

23

Otherwise, the torch will pass
to the spiritualist and telepath,
the freudian-buddhist-psychopath—
    and from this general nirvana
laws will flutter down in visions,
addicts will be fixing ribbons
on themselves. Instead of icons,
    old syringes in a corner.

24

Душу затянут большой вуалью.
Объединят нас сплошной спиралью.
Воткнут в розетку с этил-моралью.
Речь освободят от глагола.
Благодаря хорошему зелью,
закружимся в облаках каруселью.
Будем опускаться на землю
исключительно для укола.

25

Я уже вижу наш мир, который
покрыт паутиной лабораторий.
А паутиною траекторий
покрыт потолок. Как быстро!
Это неприятно для глаза.
Человечество увеличивается в три раза.
В опасности белая раса.
Неизбежно смертоубийство.

26

Либо нас перережут цветные.
Либо мы их сошлем в иные
миры. Вернемся в свои пивные.
Но то и другое—не христианство.
Православные! это не дело.
Что вы смотрите обалдело?!
Мы бы предали Божье Тело,
расчищая себе пространство.

24

Each soul, lapped in a flowing veil,
will link in a continual spiral,
live by ethyl-ethics. Speech will
 float away from Word. And thanks
to that exquisite stuff, we'll twirl
on our celestial carousel,
return to earth once in a while
 if only for another fix.

25

The world already to my eyes
is cobwebbed by laboratories.
A network of trajectories
 makes noughts-and-crosses on the clouds.
Unappealing to behold.
The population swells threefold.
The whites have lost their stranglehold.
 Murder's looking in the cards.

26

I mean, the Hordes will be the death
of us! It's either that or else
we get the bastards first. (Good health!)
 It's not exactly Christian, this,
I grant you, brothers Orthodox.
I don't know why you're looking shocked.
We all make good Iscariots
 when we decide we need the space.

27

Я не воспитывался на софистах.
Есть что-то дамское в пацифистах.
Но чистых отделять от нечистых—
не наше право, поверьте.
Я не указываю на скрижали.
Цветные нас, бесспорно, прижали.
Но не мы их на свет рожали,
не нам предавать их смерти.

28

Важно многим создать удобства.
(Это можно найти у Гоббса.)
Я сижу на стуле, считаю до ста.
Чистка—грязная процедура.
Не принято плясать на могиле.
Создать изобилие в тесном мире—
это по-христиански. Или:
в этом и состоит Культура.

29

Нынче поклонники оборота
«Религия—опиум для народа»
поняли, что им дана свобода,
дожили до золотого века.
Но в таком реестре (издержки слога)
свобода не выбрать—весьма убога.
Обычно тот, кто плюет на Бога,
плюет сначала на человека.

27

The Sophists weren't around in my day.
Pacifism's for the ladies.
But, to sift the pure from dirty
    isn't, sadly, up to us.
Nor am I Moses. Yes, the Hordes
are circling now, you mark my words,
but we didn't bring them to the earth,
    we can't arrange their exodus.

28

Comfort, then, and for us all.
(This you find in Hobbes, et al.)
I count a hundred, sitting still.
    A purge is not a nice procedure.
Vulgar, dancing on a tomb.
Wealth for our cramped world would seem
a Christian act. Or may be deemed,
    who knows, another job for Culture.

29

Now all who swallowed that old rope
"Religion is the people's opium"
know that Freedom is the dope
    whose golden air they lived to breathe.
But in their liberated modes
the freedom not to choose erodes
in squalor. One who spits at God
    will first have spattered you and me.

«Бога нет. А земля в ухабах».
«Да, не видать. Отключусь на бабах».
Творец, творящий в таких масштабах,
делает слишком большие рейды
между объектами. Так что то, что
там Его царствие—это точно.
Оно от мира сего заочно.
Сядьте на свои табуреты!

31

Ночь. Переулок. Мороз блокады.
Вдоль тротуаров лежат карпаты.
Планеты раскачиваются, как лампады,
которые Бог возжег в небосводе
в благоговеньи Своем великом
перед непознанным нами ликом
(поэзия делает смотр уликам),
как в огромном кивоте.

III

32

В Новогоднюю ночь я сижу на стуле.
Ярким блеском горят кастрюли.
Я прикладываюсь к микстуре.
Нерв разошелся, как черт в сосуде.
Ощущаю легкий пожар в затылке.
Вспоминаю выпитые бутылки,
вологодскую стражу, Кресты, Бутырки.
Не хочу возражать по сути.

30

"There is no God. The earth's a mess."
"Too right. I'll take up chicks, I guess."
So vast is His Creation, space,

    dividing objects, is too great,
the distances too wide. It's clear
His Kingdom must be *there*, not here.
It's out of sight of us, for sure.

    Nothing to see—back to your seats!

31

Night. A lane. A frost as bad
as in the siege. By every roadside,
drifts like the Carpathians. God

    has lighted in the blue immense
the planets, icon lamps to glow
before the face we cannot know.
(What's poetry but a review

    of the existing evidence?)

III

32

I sit alone on New Year's Eve.
The pans are gleaming on the shelf.
I drain a glass to my good health.

    My nerves are jumping like a djinn.
Below my skull a fire starts.
I see drained bottles, prison guards,
Vologda, Kresty, Butyrki. That's

    an old song I decline to sing.

33

Я сижу на стуле в большой квартире.
Ниагара клокочет в пустом сортире.
Я себя ощущаю мишенью в тире,
вздрагиваю при малейшем стуке.
Я закрыл парадное на засов, но
ночь в меня целит рогами Овна,
словно Амур из лука, словно
Сталин в XVII-ый съезд из «тулки».

34

Я включаю газ, согреваю кости.
Я сижу на стуле, трясусь от злости.
Не желаю искать жемчуга в компосте!
Я беру на себя эту смелость!
Пусть изучает навоз кто хочет.
Патриот, господа, не крыловский кочет.
Пусть КГБ на меня не дрочит.
Не бренчи ты в подкладке, мелочь!

35

Я дышу серебром и харкаю медью!
Меня ловят багром и дырявой сетью.
Я дразню гусей и иду к бессмертью,
дайте мне хворостину!
Я беснуюсь, как мышь в пустоте сусека!
Выносите святых и портрет Генсека!
Раздается в лесу топор дровосека!
Поваляюсь в сугробе, авось, остыну.

33

I sit in this huge place alone.
I hear Niagara in the john.
I'm target practice once again.
    Any noises make me anxious.
Night, though every door is bolted,
lowers the horns of Aries. Cupid's
Mauser's at my head, like Comrade
    Stalin's at the 17th Congress.

34

I crank the gas up, warm my bones.
I shake with anger, all alone.
No more sifting pearls in dung—
    I take this liberty! Let those
who want to study shit feel free.
A patriot isn't, pardon me,
Krylov's rooster. KGB,
    stop jerking off! Coins, hush your noise!

35

With silver breath and copper spit,
I dodge their hook and ragged net.
I stir the hornets' nest, strike out
    for immortality. My cane!
I rave, a starving mouse. Take out
the saints, take out the GenSec's portrait!
Far in the wood an ax is heard.
    I'll cool down in the snow again.

36

Ничего не остыну! Вообще забудьте!
Я помышляю почти о бунте!
Не присягал я косому Будде,
за червонец помчусь за зайцем!
Пусть закроется—где стамеска!—
яснополянская хлеборезка!
Непротивленье, панове, мерзко.
Это мне—как серпом по яйцам!

37

Как Аристотель на дне колодца,
откуда не ведаю что берется.
Зло существует, чтоб с ним бороться,
а не взвешивать в коромысле.
Всех, скорбящих по индивиду,
всех, подверженных конъюнктивиту,—
всех к той матери по алфавиту:
демократия в полном смысле!

38

Я люблю родные поля, лощины,
реки, озера, холмов морщины.
Все хорошо. Но дерьмо мужчины.
В теле, а духом слабы.
Это я верный закон накнокал.
Все утирается ясный сокол.
Господа, разбейте хоть пару стекол!
Как только терпят бабы?

36

The hell I will. Forget it, friend.
A riot's what I have in mind.
Slant-eyed Buddha's not my kind.
    Me, I'd catch a hare for peanuts.
Vegetarianism?—swing
the wrecker's ball. That lettuce gang.
Nonviolence, gents, is cattle dung.
    May as well kick me where it hurts.

37

Like Aristotle down a well,
I've no conception where the hell
things come from, but I do know Evil's
    to be fought, not figured out.
Who says the Self is history
is suffering pinkeye. Let me
suggest they line up, A to Z,
    and fuck themselves like democrats.

38

I love my native fields and dales,
the rivers, lakes, the wrinkled hills:
all very fine but men are assholes,
    strong in body, weak in spirit.
A law it takes a poet to make.
The valiant hero wipes his cheek.
Gentlemen, can you not break
    one window? How do your women stand it?

39

Грустная ночь у меня сегодня.
Смотрит с обоев былая сотня.
Можно поехать в бордель и сводня—
нумизматка—будет согласна.
Лень отклеивать, суетиться.
Остается тихо сидеть, поститься
да напротив в окно креститься,
пока оно не погасло.

40

«Зелень лета, эх, зелень лета!
Что мне шепчет куст бересклета?
Хорошо пройтись без жилета!
Зелень лета вернется.
Ходит девочка, эх, в платочке.
Ходит по полю, рвет цветочки.
Взять бы в дочки, эх, взять бы в дочки.
В небе ласточка вьется».

14 ЯНВАРЯ 1967

39

Some day I'm having here tonight.
I framed an old one-hundred note.
Might interest, say, a numismat.

 The madam's one. I could unstick
the thing. I can't be bothered. So,
I'll sit. What else is there to do?
Cross myself and face the window,
  fast until that room goes dark.

40

Sing folderol, the green of May!
What does the hedgerow sigh to me?
To walk without a shirt is my

 delight! Return, O green of May!
O, in her little scarf she'll walk
across the fields, a flower she'll pick.
I'd take her for my daughter! Look,
  a little swallow in the sky.

JANUARY 14, 1967

TRANSLATED BY GLYN MAXWELL

ANNO DOMINI

Провинция справляет Рождество.
Дворец Наместника увит омелой,
и факелы дымятся у крыльца.
В проулках—толчея и озорство.
Веселый, праздный, грязный, очумелый
народ толпится позади дворца.

Наместник болен. Лежа на одре,
покрытый шалью, взятой в Альказаре,
где он служил, он размышляет о
жене и о своем секретаре,
внизу гостей приветствующих в зале.
Едва ли он ревнует. Для него

сейчас важней замкнуться в скорлупе
болезней, снов, отсрочки перевода
на службу в Метрополию. Зане
он знает, что для праздника толпе
совсем не обязательна свобода;
по этой же причине и жене

он позволяет изменять. О чем
он думал бы, когда б его не грызли
тоска, припадки? Если бы любил?
Невольно зябко поводя плечом,
он гонит прочь пугающие мысли.
. . .Веселье в зале умеряет пыл,

ANNO DOMINI

The provinces are celebrating Christmas.
The Governor-general's mansion is bedecked
with mistletoe, torches smoke by the entrance.
In the lanes the people press and lark around.
A merry, idle, dirty, boisterous
throng crowds in the rear of the mansion.

The Governor-general is ill. He lies
on a couch, wrapped in a shawl from Alcazar,
where he once served, and his thoughts turn
on his wife and on his secretary
receiving guests downstairs in the hall.
He is not really jealous. At this moment

it's more important to him to retire
into his shell of illness, dreams, the deferment of
his transfer to the capital. And since
he knows that freedom is not needed
by the crowd at all to make a public holiday—
for this same reason he allows

even his wife to be unfaithful. What would
he think of if ennui attacks
did not plague him? If he loved?
A chilly tremor runs through his shoulders,
he chases these alarming thoughts away.
In the hall the merrymaking subsides

но все же длится. Сильно опьянев,
вожди племен стеклянными глазами
взирают в даль, лишенную врага.
Их зубы, выражавшие их гнев,
как колесо, что сжато тормозами,
застряли на улыбке, и слуга

подкладывает пищу им. Во сне
кричит купец. Звучат обрывки песен.
Жена Наместника с секретарем
выскальзывают в сад. И на стене
орел имперский, выклевавший печень
Наместника, глядит нетопырем ...

И я, писатель, повидавший свет,
пересекавший на осле экватор,
смотрю в окно на спящие холмы
и думаю о сходстве наших бед:
его не хочет видеть Император,
меня—мой сын и Цинтия. И мы,

мы здесь и сгинем. Горькую судьбу
гордыня не возвысит до улики,
что отошли от образа Творца.
Все будут одинаковы в гробу.
Так будем хоть при жизни разнолики!
Зачем куда-то рваться из дворца—

but does not end. Muddled with drink,
the leaders of the tribes stare glassily
into a distance now devoid of enemies.
Their teeth, expressive of their rage,
set in a smile that's like a wheel
held fast by brakes—and a servant

is loading them with food. In his sleep
a merchant cries out. Snatches of song are heard.
The Governor-general's wife and secretary
slip out into the garden. And on the wall
the imperial eagle, like a bat, stares down,
having gorged on the Governor-general's liver.

And I, a writer who has seen the world,
who has crossed the equator on an ass,
look out of the window at the hills asleep
and think about the identity of our woes:
the Emperor won't see him, I won't be
seen by my son and Cynthia . . . And we,

we here shall perish. Arrogance will not raise
our bitter fate to the level of proof
that we are made in the Creator's image.
The grave will render all alike.
So, if only in our lifetime, let us be various!
For what reason should we rush from the mansion,

отчизне мы не судьи. Меч суда
погрязнет в нашем собственном позоре:
наследники и власть в чужих руках . . .
Как хорошо, что не плывут суда!
Как хорошо, что замерзает море!
Как хорошо, что птицы в облаках

субтильны для столь тягостных телес!
Такого не поставишь в укоризну.
Но может быть находится как раз
к их голосам в пропорции наш вес.
Пускай летят поэтому в отчизну.
Пускай орут поэтому за нас.

Отечество . . . чужие господа
у Цинтии в гостях над колыбелью
склоняются, как новые волхвы.
Младенец дремлет. Теплится звезда,
как уголь под остывшею купелью.
И гости, не коснувшись головы,

нимб заменяют ореолом лжи,
а непорочное зачатье—сплетней,
фигурой умолчанья об отце . . .
Дворец пустеет. Гаснут этажи.
Один. Другой. И, наконец, последний.
И только два окна во всем дворце

we cannot judge our homeland. The sword of justice
will stick fast in our personal disgrace:
the heirs, the power, are in stronger hands . . .
How good that vessels are not sailing!
How good that the sea is freezing!
How good that the birds in the clouds

are too frail for such cumbrous frames!
For that, nobody is to blame.
But perhaps our weights will be
proportionate exactly to their voices.
Therefore, let them fly to our homeland.
Therefore, let them yell out to us.

My country . . . foreign gentlemen,
visiting Cynthia, are leaning
over the crib like latter-day magi.
The infant slumbers. A star glimmers
like a coal under a cold font.
And the visitors, not touching his head,

replace the halo by an aureole of lies,
and the Virgin Birth by gossip,
by the passing over of the father in silence . . .
The mansion empties. The lights on each floor die.
First one, then another. Finally, the last.
And only two windows in the whole palace

горят: мое, где, к факелу спиной,
смотрю, как диск луны по редколесью
скользит, и вижу—Цинтию, снега;
Наместника, который за стеной
всю ночь безмолвно борется с болезнью
и жжет огонь, чтоб различить врага.

Враг отступает. Жидкий свет зари,
чуть занимаясь на Востоке мира,
вползает в окна, норовя взглянуть
на то, что совершается внутри,
и, натыкаясь на остатки пира,
колеблется. Но продолжает путь.

ПАЛАНГА, ЯНВАРЬ 1968

are alight: mine, where, with my back to the torchlight,
I watch the moon's disk glide
over the sparsely growing trees, and see
Cynthia, the snow; the Governor-general's, where
he struggles silently all night with his illness
and keeps the fire lit, to see his enemy.

The enemy withdraws. The faint light of day
barely breaking in the world's East,
creeps through the window, straining
to see what is happening within,
and, coming across the remnants of the feast,
falters. But continues on its way.

PALANGA, JANUARY 1968

TRANSLATED BY DANIEL WEISSBORT

E.R.

Второе Рождество на берегу
незамерзающего Понта.
Звезда Царей над изгородью порта.
И не могу сказать, что не могу
жить без тебя—поскольку я живу.
Как видно из бумаги. Существую;
глотаю пиво, пачкаю листву и
топчу траву.

Теперь в кофейне, из которой мы,
как и пристало временно счастливым,
беззвучным были выброшены взрывом
в грядущее, под натиском зимы
бежав на Юг, я пальцами черчу
твое лицо на мраморе для бедных;
поодаль нимфы прыгают, на бедрах
задрав парчу.

Что, боги,—если бурое пятно
в окне символизирует вас, боги,—
стремились вы нам высказать в итоге?
Грядущее настало, и оно
переносимо; падает предмет,
скрипач выходит, музыка не длится,
и море все морщинистей, и лица.
А ветра нет.

A second Christmas by the shore
of Pontus, which remains unfrozen.
The Star of Kings above the sharp horizon
of harbor walls. And I can't say for sure
that I can't live without you. As
this paper proves, I do exist: I'm living
enough to gulp my beer, to soil the leaves, and
trample the grass.

Retreating south before winter's assault,
I sit in that café from which we two were
exploded soundlessly into the future
according to the unrelenting law
that happiness can't last. My finger tries
your face on poor man's marble. In the distance,
brocaded nymphs leap through their jerky dances,
flaunting their thighs.

Just what, you gods—if this dilating blot,
glimpsed through a murky window, symbolizes
your selves now—were you trying to advise us?
The future has arrived and it is not
unbearable. Things fall, the fiddler goes,
the music ebbs, and deepening creases
spread over the sea's surface and men's faces.
But no wind blows.

Когда-нибудь оно, а не—увы—
мы, захлестнет решетку променада
и двинется под возгласы «не надо»,
вздымая гребни выше головы,
туда, где ты пила свое вино,
спала в саду, просушивала блузку,
—круша столы, грядущему моллюску
готовя дно.

ЯЛТА, ЯНВАРЬ 1971

Someday the slowly rising breakers but,
alas, not we, will sweep across this railing,
crest overhead, crush helpless screams, and roll in
to find the spot where you drank wine, took cat-
naps, spreading to the sun your wet
thin blouse—to batter benches, splinter boardwalks,
and build for future molluscs
a silted bed.

YALTA, JANUARY 1971

TRANSLATED BY GEORGE L. KLINE

24 ДЕКАБРЯ 1971 ГОДА

V.S.

В Рождество все немного волхвы.
  В продовольственных слякоть и давка.
Из-за банки кофейной халвы
  производит осаду прилавка
грудой свертков навьюченный люд:
  каждый сам себе царь и верблюд.

Сетки, сумки, авоськи, кульки,
  шапки, галстуки, сбитые набок.
Запах водки, хвои и трески,
  мандаринов, корицы и яблок.
Хаос лиц, и не видно тропы
  в Вифлеем из-за снежной крупы.

И разносчики скромных даров
  в транспорт прыгают, ломятся в двери,
исчезают в провалах дворов,
  даже зная, что пусто в пещере:
ни животных, ни яслей, ни Той,
  над Которою—нимб золотой.

Пустота. Но при мысли о ней
  видишь вдруг как бы свет ниоткуда.
Знал бы Ирод, что чем он сильней,
  тем верней, неизбежнее чудо.
Постоянство такого родства—
  основной механизм Рождества.

DECEMBER 24, 1971

FOR V.S.

When it's Christmas we're all of us magi.
At the grocers' all slipping and pushing.
Where a tin of halvah, coffee-flavored,
is the cause of a human assault-wave
by a crowd heavy-laden with parcels:
each one his own king, his own camel.

Nylon bags, carrier bags, paper cones,
caps and neckties all twisted up sideways.
Reek of vodka and resin and cod,
orange mandarins, cinnamon, apples.
Floods of faces, no sign of a pathway
toward Bethlehem, shut off by blizzard.

And the bearers of moderate gifts
leap on buses and jam all the doorways,
disappear into courtyards that gape,
though they know that there's nothing inside there:
not a beast, not a crib, nor yet her,
round whose head gleams a nimbus of gold.

Emptiness. But the mere thought of that
brings forth lights as if out of nowhere.
Herod reigns but the stronger he is,
the more sure, the more certain the wonder.
In the constancy of this relation
is the basic mechanics of Christmas.

То и празднуют нынче везде,
     что Его приближенье, сдвигая
все столы. Не потребность в звезде
     пусть еще, но уж воля благая в
человеках видна издали,
     и костры пастухи разожгли.

Валит снег; не дымят, но трубят
     трубы кровель. Все лица, как пятна.
Ирод пьет. Бабы прячут ребят.
     Кто грядет—никому непонятно:
мы не знаем примет, и сердца
     могут вдруг не признать пришлеца.

Но, когда на дверном сквозняке
     из тумана ночного густого
возникает фигура в платке,
     и Младенца, и Духа Святого
ощущаешь в себе без стыда;
     смотришь в небо и видишь—звезда.

ЯНВАРЬ 1972

That's what they celebrate everywhere,
for its coming push tables together.
No demand for a star for a while,
but a sort of good will touched with grace
can be seen in all men from afar,
and the shepherds have kindled their fires.

Snow is falling: not smoking but sounding
chimney pots on the roof, every face like a stain.
Herod drinks. Every wife hides her child.
He who comes is a mystery: features
are not known beforehand, men's hearts may
not be quick to distinguish the stranger.

But when drafts through the doorway disperse
the thick mist of the hours of darkness
and a shape in a shawl stands revealed,
both a newborn and Spirit that's Holy
in your self you discover; you stare
skyward, and it's right there:

                          a star.

JANUARY 1972

TRANSLATED BY ALAN MYERS WITH THE AUTHOR

ЛАГУНА

I

Три старухи с вязаньем в глубоких креслах
толкуют в холле о муках крестных;
          пансион «Аккадемиа» вместе со
всей Вселенной плывет к Рождеству под рокот
телевизора; сунув гроссбух под локоть,
          клерк поворачивает колесо.

II

И восходит в свой номер на борт по трапу
постоялец, несущий в кармане граппу,
          совершенный никто, человек в плаще,
потерявший память, отчизну, сына;
по горбу его плачет в лесах осина,
          если кто-то плачет о нем вообще.

III

Венецийских церквей, как сервизов чайных,
слышен звон в коробке из-под случайных
          жизней. Бронзовый осьминог
люстры в трельяже, заросшем ряской,
лижет набрякший слезами, лаской,
          грязными снами сырой станок.

LAGOON

FOR BROOKE AND STROBE TALBOTT

I

Down in the lobby three elderly women, bored,
take up, with their knitting, the Passion of Our Lord
    as the universe and the tiny realm
of the *pension* Accademia, side by side,
with TV blaring, sail into Christmastide,
    a lookout desk clerk at the helm.

II

And a nameless lodger, a nobody, boards the boat,
a bottle of grappa concealed in his raincoat
    as he gains his shadowy room, bereaved
of memory, homeland, son, with only the noise
of distant forests to grieve for his former joys,
    if anyone is grieved.

III

Venetian church bells, teacups, mantel clocks
chime and confound themselves in this stale box
    of assorted lives. The brazen, coiled
octopus-chandelier appears to be licking,
in a triptych mirror, bedsheet and mattress ticking,
    sodden with tears and passion-soiled.

IV

Адриатика ночью восточным ветром
канал наполняет, как ванну, с верхом,
      лодки качает, как люльки; фиш,
а не вол в изголовьи встает ночами,
и звезда морская в окне лучами
      штору шевелит, покуда спишь.

V

Так и будем жить, заливая мертвой
водой стеклянной графина мокрый
      пламень граппы, кромсая леща, а не
птицу-гуся, чтобы нас насытил
предок хордовый Твой, Спаситель,
      зимней ночью в сырой стране.

VI

Рождество без снега, шаров и ели
у моря, стесненного картой в теле;
      створку моллюска пустив ко дну,
пряча лицо, но спиной пленяя,
Время выходит из волн, меняя
      стрелку на башне—ее одну.

VII

Тонущий город, где твердый разум
внезапно становится мокрым глазом,
      где сфинксов северных южный брат,
знающий грамоте лев крылатый,
книгу захлопнув, не крикнет «ратуй!»,
      в плеске зеркал захлебнуться рад.

IV

Blown by night winds, an Adriatic tide
floods the canals, boats rock from side to side,
      moored cradles, and the humble bream,
not ass and oxen, guards the rented bed
where the window blind above your sleeping head
      moves to the sea star's guiding beam.

V

So this is how we cope, putting out the heat
of grappa with nightstand water, carving the meat
      of flounder instead of Christmas roast,
so that Thy earliest backboned ancestor
might feed and nourish us, O Saviour,
      this winter night on a damp coast.

VI

A Christmas without snow, tinsel, or tree,
at the edge of a map- and land-corseted sea;
      having scuttled and sunk its scallop shell,
concealing its face while flaunting its backside,
Time rises from the goddess's frothy tide,
      yet changes nothing but clock hand and bell.

VII

A drowning city, where suddenly the dry
light of reason dissolves in the moisture of the eye;
      its winged lion, which can read and write,
southern kin of northern sphinxes of renown,
won't drop his book and holler, but calmly drown
      in splinters of mirror, splashing light.

VIII

Гондолу бьет о гнилые сваи.
Звук отрицает себя, слова и
      слух; а также державу ту,
где руки тянутся хвойным лесом
перед мелким, но хищным бесом
      и слюну леденит во рту.

IX

Скрестим же с левой, вобравшей когти,
правую лапу, согнувши в локте;
      жест получим, похожий на
молот в серпе—и как чорт Солохе,
храбро покажем его эпохе,
      принявшей образ дурного сна.

X

Тело в плаще обживает сферы,
где у Софии, Надежды, Веры
      и Любви нет грядущего, но всегда
есть настоящее, сколь бы горек
ни был вкус поцелуев эбре́ и гоек,
      и города, где стопа следа

XI

не оставляет, как челн на глади
водной, любое пространство сзади,
      взятое в цифрах, сводя к нулю,
не оставляет следов глубоких
на площадях, как «прощай», широких,
      в улицах узких, как звук «люблю».

VIII

The gondola knocks against its moorings. Sound
cancels itself, hearing and words are drowned,
    as is that nation where among
forests of hands the tyrant of the State
is voted in, its only candidate,
    and spit goes ice-cold on the tongue.

IX

So let us place the left paw, sheathing its claws,
in the crook of the arm of the other one, because
    this makes a hammer-and-sickle sign
with which to salute our era and bestow
a mute up-yours-even-unto-the-elbow
    upon the nightmares of our time.

X

The raincoated figure is settling into place
where Sophia, Constance, Prudence, Faith, and Grace
    lack futures, the only tense that is
is present, where either a goyish or Yiddish kiss
tastes bitter, like the city, where footsteps fade
    invisibly along the colonnade,

XI

trackless and blank as a gondola's passage through
a water surface, smoothing out of view
    the measured wrinkles of its path,
unmarked as a broad "So long!" like the wide piazza's space,
or as a cramped "I love," like the narrow alleyways,
    erased and without aftermath.

XII

Шпили, колонны, резьба, лепнина
арок, мостов и дворцов; взгляни на-
        верх: увидишь улыбку льва
на охваченной ветром, как платьем, башне,
несокрушимой, как злак вне пашни,
        с поясом времени вместо рва.

XIII

Ночь на Сан-Марко. Прохожий с мятым
лицом, сравнимым во тьме со снятым
        с безымянного пальца кольцом, грызя
ноготь, смотрит, объят покоем,
в то «никуда», задержаться в коем
        мысли можно, зрачку—нельзя.

XIV

Там, за нигде, за его пределом
—черным, бесцветным, возможно, белым—
        есть какая-то вещь, предмет.
Может быть, тело. В эпоху тренья
скорость света есть скорость зренья;
        даже тогда, когда света нет.

1973

XII

Moldings and carvings, palaces and flights
of stairs. Look up: the lion smiles from heights
    of a tower wrapped as in a coat
of wind, unbudged, determined not to yield,
like a rank weed at the edge of a plowed field,
    and girdled round by Time's deep moat.

XIII

Night in St. Mark's piazza. A face as creased
as a finger from its fettering ring released,
    biting a nail, is gazing high
into that *nowhere* of pure thought, where sight
is baffled by the bandages of night,
    serene, beyond the naked eye,

XIV

where, past all boundaries and all predicates,
black, white, or colorless, vague, volatile states,
    something, some object, comes to mind.
Perhaps a body. In our dim days and few,
the speed of light equals a fleeting view,
    even when blackout robs us blind.

1973

TRANSLATED BY ANTHONY HECHT

Замерзший кисельный берег. Прячущий в молоке
отражения город. Позвякивают куранты.
Комната с абажуром. Ангелы вдалеке
галдят, точно высыпавшие из кухни официанты.
Я пишу тебе это с другой стороны земли
в день рожденья Христа. Снежное толковище
за окном разражается искренним «ай-люли»:
белизна размножается. Скоро Ему две тыщи
лет. Осталось четырнадцать. Нынче уже среда,
завтра—четверг. Данную годовщину
нам, боюсь, отмечать не добавляя льда,
избавляя следующую морщину
от еённой щеки; в просторечии—вместе с Ним.
Вот тогда мы и свидимся. Как звезда—селянина,
через стенку пройдя, слух бередит одним
пальцем разбуженное пианино.
Будто кто-то там учится азбуке по складам.
Или нет—астрономии, вглядываясь в начертанья
личных имен там, где нас нету: там,
где сумма зависит от вычитанья.

ДЕКАБРЬ 1985

With riverbanks of frozen chocolate, a city
mixes its reflections with milk. A chiming of bells.
A room with a lampshade. Distantly
clouds burst open like kitchen doors with busy angels.
I am writing you this from the other side of the earth
on the birthday of Christ. The snow choir
outside the window recite, as if with one mouth,
their mute "ailu-li." Whiteness multiplies the air.
Soon He'll be two thousand. Just fourteen more years.
Today is Wednesday. Tomorrow Thursday. An anniversary
that we have to observe with Him without adding ice
or another wrinkle to its cheek, to put it simply.
That is when we will meet. As a star . . . a villager,
through the wall I hear
a piano woken by one finger
like someone learning the alphabet all over
or rather, astronomy, peering into the font
of the constellations for our names where we are not
and where the whole amount
depends on our subtraction into nought.

DECEMBER 1985

TRANSLATED BY DEREK WALCOTT

Снег идет, оставляя весь мир в меньшинстве.
В эту пору—разгул Пинкертонам,
и себя настигаешь в любом естестве
по небрежности оттиска в оном.
За такие открытья не требуют мзды;
тишина по всему околотку.
Сколько света набилось в осколок звезды,
на ночь глядя! как беженцев в лодку.
Не ослепни, смотри! Ты и сам сирота,
отщепенец, стервец, вне закона.
За душой, как ни шарь, ни черта. Изо рта—
пар клубами, как профиль дракона.
Помолись лучше вслух, как второй Назорей,
за бредущих с дарами в обеих
половинках земли самозваных царей
и за всех детей в колыбелях.

(1986)

Snow is falling, leaving the whole world outmanned,
in the minority. Now your private detective
agency comes into its own and
you catch up with yourself because your prints are so
                                        recognizably defective.
Not that you're about to collect a reward
for turning yourself in. A noiseless, nothing of note
precinct. With the onset of night, so much light's packed
                                        into one star-shard
it's like refugees packed into one boat.
Mind you don't go blind. You yourself are on the street,
an orphan, a social pariah, an outcast
who, for all your pocket slapping, have come up with sweet
damn all. From your mouth there issues only a dragon blast
of hot air. Maybe the time has come for you, another
                                        Nazarene, to offer
up a prayer for all those hotshot
wise men, from both sides of the planet, schlepping along
                                        with their groaning coffers,
for all the little children in their carry cots.

(1986)

TRANSLATED BY PAUL MULDOON

РОЖДЕСТВЕНСКАЯ ЗВЕЗДА

В холодную пору, в местности, привычной скорей к
                                                            жаре,
чем к холоду, к плоской поверхности более, чем к горе,
младенец родился в пещере, чтоб мир спасти;
мело, как только в пустыне может зимой мести.

Ему все казалось огромным; грудь матери, желтый пар
из воловьих ноздрей, волхвы—Бальтазар, Каспар,
Мельхиор; их подарки, втащенные сюда.
Он был всего лишь точкой. И точка была звезда.

Внимательно, не мигая, сквозь редкие облака,
на лежащего в яслях ребенка издалека,
из глубины Вселенной, с другого ее конца,
звезда смотрела в пещеру. И это был взгляд отца.

24 ДЕКАБРЯ 1987

STAR OF THE NATIVITY

In the cold season, in a locality accustomed to heat more
                                                                than
to cold, to horizontality more than to a mountain,
a child was born in a cave in order to save the world;
it blew as only in deserts in winter it blows, athwart.

To Him, all things seemed enormous: His mother's breast,
                                                                the steam
out of the ox's nostrils, Caspar, Balthazar, Melchior—the team
of Magi, their presents heaped by the door, ajar.
He was but a dot, and a dot was the star.

Keenly, without blinking, through pallid, stray
clouds, upon the child in the manger, from far away—
from the depth of the universe, from its opposite end—the star
was looking into the cave. And that was the Father's stare.

DECEMBER 24, 1987

TRANSLATED BY THE AUTHOR

БЕГСТВО В ЕГИПЕТ

... погонщик возник неизвестно откуда.

В пустыне, подобранной небом для чуда,
по принципу сходства, случившись ночлегом,
они жгли костер. В заметаемой снегом
пещере, своей не предчувствуя роли,
младенец дремал в золотом ореоле
волос, обретавших стремительно навык
свеченья—не только в державе чернявых,
сейчас, но и вправду подобно звезде,
покуда земля существует: везде.

25 ДЕКАБРЯ 1988

FLIGHT INTO EGYPT

. . . where the drover came from, no one knew.

Their affinity made the heavens slate
the desert for a miracle. There, they chose to light
a fire and camp, the cave in a vortex of snow.
Not divining his role, the Infant drowsed
in a halo of curls that would quickly become
accustomed to radiance. Its glow would climb—
beyond that dark-skinned enclave—to rise
like the light of a star that endures
as long as the earth exists: everywhere.

DECEMBER 25, 1988

TRANSLATED BY MELISSA GREEN

Представь, чиркнув спичкой, тот вечер в пещере,
используй, чтоб холод почувствовать, щели
в полу, чтоб почувствовать голод—посуду,
а что до пустыни, пустыня повсюду.

Представь, чиркнув спичкой, ту полночь в пещере,
огонь, очертанья животных, вещей ли,
и—складкам смешать дав лицо с полотенцем—
Марию, Иосифа, сверток с Младенцем.

Представь трех царей, караванов движенье
к пещере; верней, трех лучей приближенье
к звезде, скрип поклажи, бренчание ботал
(Младенец покамест не заработал

на колокол с эхом в сгустившейся сини).
Представь, что Господь в Человеческом Сыне
впервые Себя узнает на огромном
впотьмах расстояньи: бездомный в бездомном.

1989

Imagine striking a match that night in the cave:
use the cracks in the floor to feel the cold.
Use crockery in order to feel the hunger.
And to feel the desert—but the desert is everywhere.

Imagine striking a match in that midnight cave,
the fire, the farm beasts in outline, the farm tools and stuff;
and imagine, as you towel your face in the towel's folds,
the bundled up Infant. And Mary and Joseph.

Imagine the kings, the caravans' stilted procession
as they make for the cave, or rather three beams closing in
and in on the star; the creaking of loads, the clink of a
                                                    cowbell;
(but in the cerulean thickening over the Infant

no bell and no echo of bell: He hasn't yet earned it.)
Imagine the Lord, for the first time, from darkness, and
                                                    stranded
immensely in distance, recognizing Himself in the Son
of Man: homeless, going out to Himself in a homeless one.

1989

TRANSLATED BY SEAMUS HEANEY

Неважно, что было вокруг, и неважно,
о чем там пурга завывала протяжно,
что тесно им было в пастушьей квартире,
что места другого им не было в мире.

Во-первых, они были вместе. Второе,
и главное, было, что их было трое,
и все, что творилось, варилось, дарилось,
отныне, как минимум, на три делилось.

Морозное небо над ихним привалом
с привычкой большого склоняться над малым
сверкало звездою—и некуда деться
ей было отныне от взгляда младенца.

Костер полыхал, но полено кончалось;
все спали. Звезда от других отличалась
сильней, чем свеченьем, казавшимся лишним,
способностью дальнего смешивать с ближним.

25 ДЕКАБРЯ 1990

NATIVITY

No matter what went on around them; no matter
what message the snowstorm was straining to utter;
or how crowded they thought that wooden affair;
or that there was nothing for them anywhere;

first, they were together. And—most of all—second,
they now were a threesome. Whatever was reckoned—
the stuff they were brewing, accruing, receiving—
was bound to be split into three, like this evening.

Above their encampment, the sky, cold and idle,
and leaning as big things will do over little,
was burning a star, which from this very instant
had no place to go, save the gaze of the infant.

The campfire flared on its very last ember.
They all were asleep now. The star would resemble
no other, because of its knack, at its nadir,
for taking an alien for its neighbor.

DECEMBER 25, 1990

TRANSLATED BY THE AUTHOR

PRESEPIO

Младенец, Мария, Иосиф, цари,
скотина, верблюды, их поводыри,
в овчине до пят пастухи-исполины
—все стало набором игрушек из глины.

В усыпанном блестками ватном снегу
пылает костер. И потрогать фольгу
звезды пальцем хочется; собственно, всеми
пятью—как младенцу тогда в Вифлееме.

Тогда в Вифлееме все было крупней.
Но глине приятно с фольгою над ней
и ватой, разбросанной тут как попало,
играть роль того, что из виду пропало.

Теперь ты огромней, чем все они. Ты
теперь с недоступной для них высоты
—полночным прохожим в окошко конурки—
из космоса смотришь на эти фигурки.

Там жизнь продолжается, так как века
одних уменьшают в объеме, пока
другие растут—как случилось с тобою.
Там бьются фигурки со снежной крупою,

PRESEPIO

The wise men; Joseph; the tiny Infant; Mary;
the cows; the drovers, each with his dromedary;
the hulking shepherds in their sheepskins—they
have all become toy figures made of clay.

In the cotton-batting snow that's strewn with glints,
a fire is blazing. You'd like to touch that tinsel
star with a finger—or all five of them,
as the infant wished to do in Bethlehem.

All this, in Bethlehem, was of greater size.
Yet the clay, round which the drifted cotton lies,
with tinsel overhead, feels good to be
enacting what we can no longer see.

Now you are huge compared to them, and high
beyond their ken. Like a midnight passerby
who finds the pane of some small hut aglow,
you peer from the cosmos at this little show.

There life goes on, although the centuries
require that some diminish by degrees,
while others grow, like you. The small folk there
contend with granular snow and icy air,

и самая меньшая пробует грудь.
И тянет зажмуриться, либо—шагнуть
в другую галактику, в гулкой пустыне
которой светил—как песку в Палестине.

ДЕКАБРЬ 1991

and the smallest reaches for the breast, and you
half wish to clench your eyes, or step into
a different galaxy, in whose wastes there shine
more lights than there are sands in Palestine.

DECEMBER 1991

TRANSLATED BY RICHARD WILBUR

КОЛЫБЕЛЬНАЯ

Родила тебя в пустыне
      я не зря.
Потому что нет в помине
      в ней царя.

В ней искать тебя напрасно.
      В ней зимой
стужи больше, чем пространства
      в ней самой.

У одних—игрушки, мячик,
      дом высок.
У тебя для игр ребячьих
      —весь песок.

Привыкай, сынок, к пустыне
      как к судьбе.
Где б ты ни был, жить отныне
      в ней тебе.

Я тебя кормила грудью.
      А она
приучила взгляд к безлюдью,
      им полна.

Той звезде, на расстояньи
      страшном, в ней
твоего чела сиянье,
      знать, видней.

LULLABY

Birth I gave you in a desert
not by chance,
for no king would ever hazard
its expanse.

Seeking you in it, I figure,
won't be wise
since its winter cold is bigger
than its size.

As you suck my breast, this vastness,
all this width,
feeds your gaze the human absence
it's filled with.

Grow accustomed to the desert
as to fate,
lest you find it omnipresent
much too late.

Some get toys, in piles and layers,
wrapped or bound.
You, my baby, have to play with
all the sand.

See that star, at terrifying
height, aglow?
Say, this void just helps it, eyeing
you below.

Привыкай, сынок, к пустыне.
Под ногой,
окромя нее, твердыни
нет другой.

В ней судьба открыта взору.
За версту.
В ней легко признаешь гору
по кресту.

Не людские, знать, в ней тропы!
Велика
и безлюдна она, чтобы
шли века.

Привыкай, сынок, к пустыне,
как щепоть
к ветру, чувствуя, что ты не
только плоть.

Привыкай жить с этой тайной:
чувства те
пригодятся, знать, в бескрайней
пустоте.

Не хужей она, чем эта:
лишь длинней,
и любовь к тебе—примета
места в ней.

Grow accustomed to the desert.
Uniform
underfoot, for all it isn't,
it's most firm.

In it, fate rejects a phantom
faint or gross:
one can tell for miles a mountain
by a cross.

Paths one sees here are not really
human paths
but the centuries' which freely
through it pass.

Grow accustomed to the desert:
flesh is not—
as the speck would sigh, wind-pestered—
all you've got.

Keep this secret, child, for later.
That, I guess,
may just help you in a greater
emptiness.

Which is like this one, just ever-
lasting; and
in it love for you shows where
it might end.

Привыкай к пустыне, милый,
и к звезде,
льющей свет с такою силой
в ней везде,

точно лампу жжет, о сыне
в поздний час
вспомнив, тот, кто сам в пустыне
дольше нас.

ДЕКАБРЬ 1992

Grow accustomed to the desert
and the star
pouring down its incandescent
rays, which are

just a lamp to guide the treasured
child who's late,
lit by someone whom that desert
taught to wait.

DECEMBER 1992

TRANSLATED BY THE AUTHOR

25. XII. 1993

Что нужно для чуда? Кожух овчара,
щепотка сегодня, крупица вчера,
и к пригоршне завтра добавь на глазок
огрызок пространства и неба кусок.

И чудо свершится. Зане чудеса
к земле тяготея, хранят адреса,
настолько добраться стремясь до конца,
что даже в пустыне находят жильца.

А если ты дом покидаешь — включи
звезду на прощанье в четыре свечи
чтоб мир без вещей освещала она,
вослед тебе глядя, во все времена.

1993

25.XII.1993

TO M.V.

For a miracle, take one shepherd's sheepskin, throw
in a pinch of now, a grain of long ago,
and a handful of tomorrow. Add by eye
a little chunk of space, a piece of sky,

and it will happen. For miracles, gravitating
to earth, know just where people will be waiting,
and eagerly will find the right address
and tenant, even in a wilderness.

Or if you're leaving home, switch on a new
four-pointed star, then, as you say adieu,
to light a vacant world with steady blaze
and follow you forever with its gaze.

1993

TRANSLATED BY RICHARD WILBUR

В воздухе—сильный мороз и хвоя.
Наденем ватное и меховое.
Чтоб мыкаться в наших сугробах с торбой—
лучше олень, чем верблюд двугорбый.

На севере если и верят в Бога,
то как в коменданта того острога,
где всем нам вроде бока намяло,
но только и слышно, что дали мало.

На юге, где в редкость осадок белый,
верят в Христа, так как сам он—беглый:
родился в пустыне, песок-солома,
и умер тоже, слыхать, не дома.

Помянем нынче вином и хлебом
жизнь, прожитую под открытым небом,
чтоб в нем и потом избежать ареста
земли—поскольку там больше места.

ДЕКАБРЬ 1994

The air—fierce frost and pine-boughs.
We'll cram ourselves in thick clothes,
stumbling in drifts till we're weary—
better a reindeer than a dromedary.

In the North if faith does not fail
God appears as the warden of a jail
where the kicks in our ribs were rough
but what you hear is "They didn't get enough."

In the South the white stuff's a rare sight,
they love Christ who was also in flight,
desert-born, sand and straw his welcome,
he died, so they say, far from home.

So today, commemorate with wine and bread,
a life with just the sky's roof overhead
because up there a man escapes
the arresting earth—plus there's more space.

DECEMBER 1994

TRANSLATED BY DEREK WALCOTT

БЕГСТВО В ЕГИПЕТ (2)

В пещере (какой ни на есть, а кров!
Надежней суммы прямых углов!)
в пещере им было тепло втроем;
пахло соломою и тряпьем.

Соломенною была постель.
Снаружи молола песок метель.
И, вспоминая её помол,
спросонья ворочались мул и вол.

Мария молилась; костер гудел.
Иосиф, насупясь, в огонь глядел.
Младенец, будучи слишком мал
чтоб делать что-то еще, дремал.

Еще один день позади—с его
тревогами, страхами; с «о-го-го»
Ирода, выславшего войска;
и ближе еще на один—века.

Спокойно им было в ту ночь втроем.
Дым устремлялся в дверной проем,
чтоб не тревожить их. Только мул
во сне (или вол) тяжело вздохнул.

FLIGHT INTO EGYPT (2)

In the cave—it sheltered them, at least,
safer than four square-set right angles—
in the cave the threesome felt secure
in the reek of straw and old clobber.

Straw for bedding. Outside the door,
blizzard, sandstorm, howling air.
Mule rubbed ox; they stirred and groaned
like sand and snowflake scourged in wind.

Mary prays; the fire soughs;
Joseph frowns into the blaze.
Too small to be fit to do a thing
but sleep, the infant is just sleeping.

Another day behind them now,
its worries past. And the "ho, ho, ho!"
of Herod who had sent the troops.
And the centuries a day closer too.

That night, as three, they were at peace.
Smoke like a retiring guest
slipped out the door. There was one far-off
heavy sigh from the mule. Or the ox.

Звезда глядела через порог.
Единственным среди них, кто мог
знать, что взгляд ее означал,
был младенец; но он молчал.

ДЕКАБРЬ 1995

The star looked in across the threshold.
The only one of them who could
know the meaning of that look
was the infant. But He did not speak.

DECEMBER 1995

TRANSLATED BY SEAMUS HEANEY

A Conversation with Joseph Brodsky

PETER VAIL

PV: Joseph, Biblical stories and characters appear consistently in your poems (though less often than images of ancient Rome and Greece). At least a couple of dozen poems concern the Nativity. What explains such attention to this subject?

JB: Above all, this is a temporal holiday, linked to a particular reality, to the movement of time. In the final analysis, what is the Nativity? The birthday of God-made-man. And it's no less natural for humans to celebrate it than for them to celebrate their own.

PV: The first Christmas poem included in your collections is from 1962, "Christmas Ballad," with a dedication to [the Russian poet] Evgeny Rein.

JB: Ever since I took to writing poems seriously—more or less seriously—I've tried to write a poem for every Christmas—as a sort of birthday greeting. Several times I've missed the opportunity, let it slip by. One or another circumstance blocked the road.

PV: Outsiders can only speculate about personal motives, but any reader can make judgments about a poet's cosmology. You clearly are more interested in time than in space. Christianity itself, in contrast to Eastern religions, for example, structures time. One can first of all affirm as definitive the historical fact of the Nativity, a universal point of departure.

JB: This kind of, how to put it, historical temerity, is inherent in every religious doctrine. We have the category B.C., that is, "before the birth of Christ." What is included in this "before"? Not only, let's say, Caesar Augustus or his ancestors, but all the geological periods, going back at that end practically into astronomy. This has always rather overwhelmed me. What is remarkable about

Christmas? The fact that what we're dealing with here is the calculation of life—or, at the very least, existence—in the consciousness of an individual, of a specific individual.

PV: Joseph, your Christmas poems of 1988 to 1990 are written in one particular meter. In earlier poems one found iambs, anapests, and variably stressed *dolniks*, then these four poems are written in a classic four-foot amphibrach (the meter of Pasternak's poem "Star of the Nativity," by the way). Is this a coincidence or does it indicate a certain stability, the strengthening of a tradition?

JB: I think it's rather a sign of a particular tonality. What attracts me in the amphibrach is that it exhibits a certain monotony. It gets rid of accents. It gets rid of bathos. It's an absolutely neutral meter.

PV: The meter of speech?

JB: Narrative. It narrates . . . not exactly in a lazy way, but with a kind of displeasure in regard to the process. This meter, as I see it, possesses the intonation inherent in time itself. It goes without saying that the same effect can be achieved in iambs as well, and in hexameters, and in other meters, if you are clever enough. But monotony is natural here. Moreover, these poems are written in couplets, so to speak. The usual form for popular verse. Crudely speaking, an imitation of folklore.

PV: Form is of course linked to content. Your poems of the 1960s and '70s resemble fantasies on the theme of Christmas. In several of them, for example, in "Speech over Spilled Milk," the subject departs strongly from the first line—"I arrive at Christmas without a kopeck." One could say that earlier you wrote poems on the occasion of Christmas, and in recent years you've written poems about Christmas. Correspondingly, the form has become neutral, as you put it. Is the subject itself such that it doesn't require refinements?

JB: That's right, one doesn't have to show off. At any rate, the reader—I don't know who this reader is—but at any rate he should not find this text particularly difficult.

PV: I remember I once saw at your house an artist bring you a series of prints as a present. The theme was Christ's Passion—they were done as a grotesque, the action taking place in contemporary Jerusalem, in modern dress. It was all very professional, well done, and not without flair. But as I recall, you couldn't conceal your irritation.

JB: The most unpleasant thing in all this is when a person tries to impose his own personal drama on Biblical, in particular Gospel subjects. That is, there's something narcissistic, egotistical about it, isn't there? When a contemporary artist starts turning himself inside out, demonstrating his wonderful technique at the expense of this subject, I always find it unpleasant. Here you come up against an instance where the lesser is interpreting the greater.

PV: The drama of just a human being—let's say Ovid, or, to take it further, a character, like Hamlet, for example—these are also great collisions. According to that logic one can't drag in one's own drama there either.

JB: Yes you can. And you can drag your own to Gospel subjects as well. But there's always a colossal element of bad taste here. Well, I was just brought up that way, or, rather, I brought myself up that way. When you come into contact with drama and a hero, you always have to try to understand how it was for him, and not how it is for you. Often a poet writes a poem on the death of so-and-so and usually expounds his own weltschmerz; he feels sorry for himself. He quickly loses sight of the person who is lost, and, if tears are shed, they are often because he himself is doomed to meet the same fate. This is all in extraordinarily bad taste, it's not even bad taste, it's just swinishness in a, well . . .

PV: . . . metaphysical sense.

JB: Well, yes.

PV: If it's swinishness, then specifically and only in a metaphysical sense, because on a purely everyday, human level, it's quite understandable.

JB: In a human sense it's natural, but even in a human sense it winds up that you don't love the one who is gone, but yourself; that you don't pity him, but yourself. In my opinion, one should always pity someone else more. That's how it seems to me, though perhaps it's a matter of temperament, no? For example, I would never stand up for myself, but for someone else—you always intercede. I had no problem excusing the Soviet authorities insofar as they slapped me around—that is, I couldn't care less, I think I deserved it all. But when they slap someone else around in front of me, that is impossible to accept. I'm not even talking about Christianity; this is, in general, pre-Christian stuff. Some Christian I am anyway.

PV: At any rate, you're not Orthodox. Your Christmas is December 25, not January 7.

JB: The response to that is simple. The tradition of celebrating Christmas is much more diverse and developed in the Roman church than it is in the Russian Orthodox. So for me there isn't the question—is it "theirs" or "not theirs"? There, where everything started, is where everything starts.

PV: That is, your attitude to this, if it can be put this way, is Christian in general.

JB: You could put it that way. I'll tell you how it all started. I wrote the first Nativity poems, I think, in Komarovo. I was living at a dacha, I don't remember whose, though it might have been Academician [Aksel] Berg's. And there I cut a picture out of a Polish magazine, I think it was *Przekrój*. The picture was *Adoration of the Magi*, I don't remember by whom. I stuck it on the ceramic stove and often looked at it in the evenings. It burned later on, the painting, and the stove, and the dacha itself. But at the time I kept on looking and decided to write a poem on the same subject. That is, it all began not from religious feelings, or from Pasternak or Eliot, but from a painting.

PV: What picture, what visual image is connected to Christmas for you now? Nature, or a cityscape?

JB: Nature, of course. For a whole series of reasons, above all because we're talking about an organic phenomenon, a natural one. Moreover, since it's connected to painting for me, the city rarely appears in the Christmas story. When the backdrop is nature, the phenomenon becomes more . . . eternal, I suppose. At least, more outside of time.

PV: I asked about the city, remembering you saying that you like to celebrate that day in Venice.

JB: The most important thing there is water—not a direct connection with Christmas, but with chronos, with time.

PV: It reminds one of that very same point of departure?

JB: Of that one, and of the water itself, as it's said, "The spirit of God moved upon the face of the waters." And was reflected in them to some extent—all these little wrinkles and so on. So at Christmas it's pleasant to look at water, and nowhere is that more pleasant than in Venice.

PV: When you have water all around, terra firma is even more important. At first the whole situation apparently seemed fairly exotic—I'm judging by the 1973 Venetian poem: "A Christmas without snow, tinsel, or tree, / at the edge of a map- and land-corseted sea." So you found something more crucial than tinsel. For that matter, there couldn't have been any tinsel, or any trees or snow in the original event, or in that painting above the ceramic stove in Komarovo. So what was it that so drew you to the painting?

JB: You know, in psychiatry there's a concept called the "capuchon" complex. A person tries to fence himself off from the world, pulls a hood over himself, and sits down, hunched over. In that painting and in other such paintings, that element is present—above all because of the cave, right? That's the way it seemed to me. In general, everything began, as I told you, not from religious considerations, but from aesthetic ones. Or psychological. I just liked that hood, I liked that concentration of everything in one place—which is what you have in the cave scene. In this regard—it goes without saying that it's pointless to argue over this—I even have some objections to Pasternak's treatment of this subject, specifically to the "Star of the Nativity."

PV: I think this is the third time that Pasternak's name has come up in the conversation, which is natural—no one else in Russian twentieth-century poetry has given so much attention to Gospel themes. You know this better than anyone: it's no coincidence, I believe, that you also have a poem called, like Pasternak's, "Star of the Nativity." What are your objections to Pasternak?

JB: There's a centrifugal force at work in his poem. The radius keeps widening out from the central figure, from the Child. While, in essence, it's all the other way around.

PV: Your movement is centripetal. In the poem of 1989 this is expressed unambiguously, although paradoxically: "three beams closing in / and in on the star," rather than the movement of the rays out from the star.

JB: That's exactly right. That is, I don't want to say that I'm right. But that's the way it seems to me, no?

PV: Your approach to Gospel themes, you say, is generally Christian, but the concentration on the Nativity—is already a kind of choice. After all, in Western Christianity this is the main, favorite holiday, and in Eastern Christianity—it's Easter.

JB: Therein you have the whole difference between the East and the West. Between us and them. We have the pathos of tears. The main idea of Easter is tears.

PV: It seems to me the primary difference is between Western rationalism and Eastern mysticism. It's one thing to be born—everyone is born—but being resurrected is another thing entirely: that's a miracle.

JB: Yes, yes, that too. But at the foundation of everything—is the pure joy of the Nativity and . . .

PV: And joy through suffering.

JB: And joy through suffering. That's why Pasternak has far more stunning poems—the [two] poems about the Crucifixion, about Magdalen. These are marvelous poems, the end [of the pair] is completely fantastic. In Pasternak, that poet of the microcosm, in his Nativity poem and in the two about Magdalen, all the movement is counter to his nature, to what we always find in him. In the Gospel poems, as I already said, the movement is centrifugal. So much so that he goes beyond the limits of doctrine. As, for instance, when he writes [speaking as Mary Magdalen], "your arms flung wide upon the cross / embrace too many in their reach."

PV: Here, of course, the words "too many" are "too much."

JB: It's heresy, if you will. But here you have the centrifugal force of the poem. The thing that's wonderful about literature is that in using religious material the metaphysical appetite of the poet or of the poem itself grows beyond the metaphysical appetite of doctrine as such. What is it that's happening in "Magdalen"? According to doctrine, Christ is resurrected. But the poem itself dictates—the lines add up and acquire a mass, which demands the next movement, a widening out.

PV: By definition doctrine narrows, limits.

JB: The poem doesn't fit within its limits. The same thing happens, let's say, with the *Divine Comedy*—this world is larger than the world dictated by the subject.

PV: But in Pasternak's "Star of the Nativity" there isn't any such heretical exit beyond the limits.

JB: There is another kind of broadening there. I think that the source of that poem is the same as mine, specifically, Italian painting. Aesthetically, the poem reminds me of Mantegna or Bellini, there are all of these circles, ellipsoids, arcs: You hear them in all the *o*s, *ah*s, and *ob*s of the fourth stanza. If you put it together with our native aesthetic, then, of course, you have an icon. All these halos are always being formed, expanding outward. There are a lot of things in Pasternak's Nativity poem—Italian painting, and Brueghel, dogs running around, et cetera, et cetera. There's a Zamoskvorechian landscape as well. Savrasov peeps through. [Zamoskvorechia is a neighborhood in Moscow, not far from the Kremlin, which is known for its churches; Aleksei Savrasov's *The Rooks Have Arrived* (1871) is one of the best-known nineteenth-century Russian paintings.—*Trans.*]

PV: At any rate, there are rooks: "Nests of rooks and the tops of trees."

JB: The source of Pasternak's cycle, and the source, to a certain extent, of this particular appeal—although I'm doing something entirely impermissible: making guesses about his religious sensations—I think that the source was Italian painting above all. It's quite possible it was a book with illustrations.

PV: Like the one you looked at?

JB: That's right, that's right. But it's just as possible that I'm mistaken.

PV: In the twentieth century there was another Russian writer who worked closely with the Gospel theme—Bulgakov.

JB: That gentleman impresses me far less than anyone else.

PV: Than anyone else writing on this subject?

JB: Than any other well-known Russian prose writer. That goes for everything except his "Theatrical Novel." As far as the Gospels are concerned, it's all largely a paraphrase of [the poet and critic Dmitry] Merezhkovsky and the literature of that time. The best thing I can say about it is that it's a good collage. And then, Bulgakov compromised himself terribly with all his amusements with the devil.

PV: In your opinion, who in Russian literature has dealt successfully with the Gospel, with Biblical subjects?

JB: Perhaps [Fyodor] Sologub. [Mikhail] Lomonosov and [Vasily] Trediakovsky have marvelous renditions. But I can't think offhand. There's Pasternak, of course. But in general there's no applied, so to speak, tradition in our literature. Religious affairs were mediated by life itself, they were a part of life, and perhaps no one thought of sitting down to write poems on a specific holiday. True, things are a bit better where Easter's concerned.

PV: In your essay "Flight from Byzantium," you expressed, in no uncertain terms, your favorable view of polytheism as compared with monotheism, and you extrapolated worldviews and social structures from them, democracy and authoritarianism, respectively. To quote you: "Polytheism was synonymous with democracy. Absolute power—autocracy—was synonymous, alas, with monotheism."

JB: I still see things the same way. In general, I think that the conflict between polytheism and monotheism is, perhaps, one of the most tragic circumstances in the history of culture. I think that in essence there really is no such conflict—especially if you consider the form it took. There were two or three people in world history who tried to surmount this. There was Julian the Apostate, and in poetry Constantine Cavafy tried to do something similar. He has six or seven poems about Julian the Apostate. For the Greeks the idea of the Trinity was an unfortunate narrowing of amplitude.

PV: An impoverished Olympus?

JB: Something like that. Simplified metaphysics.

PV: Forgive me for a personal question: are you a religious person, a believer?

JB: I don't know. Sometimes yes, sometimes no.

PV: Not a churchgoer, that's for certain.

JB: That's most definitely for certain.

PV: Not Russian Orthodox and not a Catholic either. Perhaps some sort of Protestant?

JB: Calvinist. But in fact only someone who's strongly convinced of these things can talk about them. I'm not firmly convinced of anything.

PV: Either firmly convinced or shameless.

JB: I think I'd put myself in the last category rather than in any of the previous ones. There's much in Protestantism that I dislike intensely as well. Why I say Calvinist—not particularly seriously— is because according to Calvinist doctrine man answers to himself for everything. That is, he is his own Judgment Day, to some extent. I don't have the strength to forgive myself. And, on the other hand, I don't feel any particular attraction or respect for anyone who could forgive me. When I was younger, I tried to figure this all out for myself. But at some point I realized that I am the sum of all my actions, my acts, and not the sum of my intentions.

TRANSLATED BY JAMEY GAMBRELL

Editor's Note

The translations in this book by Anthony Hecht, George L. Kline, Alan Myers, and Daniel Weissbort were made in collaboration with the author; "Lagoon" was made from an interlinear version by Stephen White. All other translations except "Christmas Ballad" were made from interlinear versions by Alexander Sumerkin, in consultation with Maria Brodsky, Margo Picken, Barry Rubin, and Masha Vorobiov. "Christmas Ballad" and "Speech over Spilled Milk" were translated in consultation with Catherine Ciepela and Tatyana Babyonyshev. We wish also to thank Lev L. Loseff.

Some of these poems have appeared in *The New Yorker*, *The New York Review of Books*, *The New York Times Book Review*, *The New Republic*, the *Los Angeles Times Book Review*, and *Threepenny Review*.

We alert the reader that "Christmas" and "Nativity" are the same word in Russian.

We wish to dedicate this English edition of *Nativity Poems* to the memory of Masha Vorobiov.

ANN KJELLBERG, DECEMBER 2001